ENGINEERING P⊙WER!

MACHINES
ON LAND

Kay Barnham

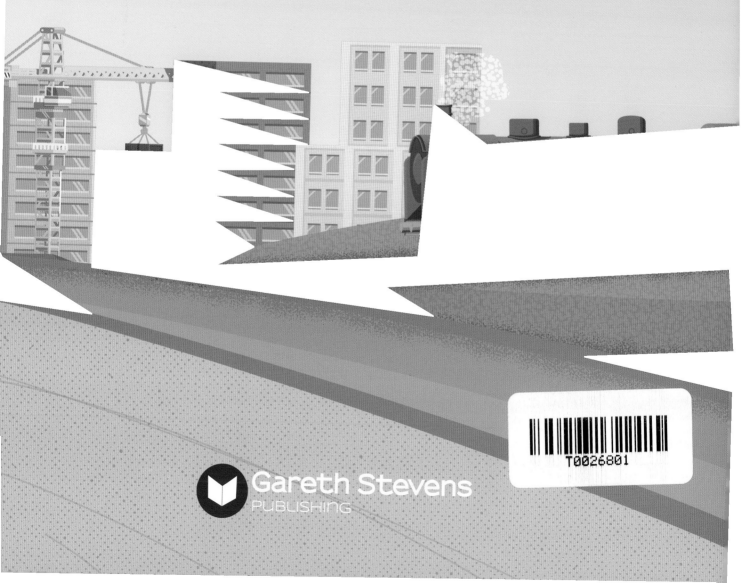

Gareth Stevens
PUBLISHING

Please visit our website, www.garethstevens.com. For a free color catalog of all our high-quality books, call toll free 1-800-542-2595 or fax 1-877-542-2596.

Cataloging-in-Publication Data

Names: Barnham, Kay.
Title: Machines on land / Kay Barnham.
Description: New York : Gareth Stevens Publishing, 2023. | Series: Engineering power! | Includes glossary and index.
Identifiers: ISBN 9781538277652 (pbk.) | ISBN 9781538277676 (library bound) | ISBN 9781538277669 (6pack) | ISBN 9781538277683 (ebook)
Subjects: LCSH: Motor vehicles--Juvenile literature.
Classification: LCC TL147.B376 2023 | DDC 629.222--dc23

Published in 2023 by
Gareth Stevens Publishing
29 E. 21st Street
New York, NY 10010

Editor: Elise Short
Design and illustration: Collaborate

Picture Credits
Alamy: dpa picture alliance 17b; OTBimages 21b. Yuriy Brykalo/Dreamstime: 19b. ETA Media Gallery/Bas de Meijer/AeroVelo: 7t. Getty Images: Norm Betts/Bloomberg 28t;David Madison 9b. KSA/NASA: 29b. LOC, Washington DC/ggbain: 14t. Courtesy of MHI Vestas Offshore Wind: 28b. Shutterstock: Jason Benz Bennee 29t; Neale Cousland 11b; cyo bo 13t; Igor Golovniov 12t; HodagMedia 6t; Levranii 26t; marekulliasz 27t; Pi-Lens 24b; rsooll 19t; Milos Stojanovic 17t; Sutipong 23t; Wlad Go 25b. Wikimedia Commons: Martin Dürrschnabel/CC 11t; Rheinische Gasmotorenfabrik Benz & Cie/PD 8t; Thames Tunnel shield contemporary image 18th century/PD: 20t; US Army/PD: 15b.

Printed in the United States of America

CPSIA compliance information: Batch #CSGS23: For further information contact Gareth Stevens, New York, New York at 1-800-542-2595.

Find us on

Contents

WHAT DO ENGINEERS DO?

Engineers use science, technology and math to find ways of doing countless different things. So whether it's whizzing around the world, diving beneath the waves, tunneling under the seabed or zooming to the Moon, it's engineers who make that happen.

MACHINES ON LAND

Engineers often design and build a machine to do a certain job. Cars, bikes, trucks and trains are machines invented by engineers so people can travel over land. But before engineers can even begin to design a machine, they have to decide what they want that machine to do. Does it need to move quickly? Will it carry a heavy load? Is it going to carry hundreds of passengers or just one? Once they have the answers to these questions—and many more—they can start work!

Top raili
for luggag
or to provid
extra seating

A stagecoach

The rear trunk is a leather-covered shelf for holding luggage, packages and mail.

The strong wooden wheels are fitted with iron rims to survive different terrains.

Throughbraces are leather straps on which the carriage rests, providing comfortable suspension.

A STAGECOACH AND HORSES

The wheel was invented 5,500 years ago. And, once people realized that a wheel was the perfect way to make something move, carts were invented too. These were pulled by animals.

Thousands of years later, animals were still being used to power vehicles. And by the 17th century, horse-drawn carriages carried people on long journeys that were broken down into stages, which is how they became known as stagecoaches. It wasn't a comfortable journey, but it meant that it took just days to travel hundreds of miles, rather than much, much longer on foot.

The driver's seat is high up to give a clear view above the horses.

The brake is operated by a foot lever and used to control speed.

Turn the page to find out all about other wonderful machines that engineering power has made possible …

BICYCLES

Did you know that bicycles are machines? They use levers, pulleys, wheels and axles to turn human power into movement. They use zero fuel, don't pollute the environment, and help riders to stay fit and healthy. They are also very, very efficient. Cyclists can go a long way using just a little energy. Even better, hardly any energy is wasted!

Popular in the 1800s, the penny-farthing's pedals were fixed to the big front wheel, so a single push made it go a long way.

Derailleurs are devices that move the chain between one set of gears and another.

The mudguard stops the rider being splattered with mud.

ALL THE GEARS!

Invented in the 19th century, the very first bicycles had iron frames and wooden wheels. They were nicknamed "boneshakers" because that's literally what they did. Meanwhile, they didn't have brakes, gears, shock-absorbers or steering. Now, bicycles are much more advanced—and safer too.

Gears allow cyclists to keep pedaling at the same rate, while spinning the wheels at different speeds. A low gear means that the bicycle moves just a short distance every time the pedals turn. This makes it easier to go up hills. Higher gears move the bicycle increasingly longer distances every time the pedals turn. The highest gears are useful when traveling on flat ground or downhill.

EXTREME ENGINEERING!

It might look like an egg-shaped spaceship, but Eta is actually a reclining bicycle built inside a shell. In 2016, it became the fastest human-powered vehicle in the world thanks to its smooth, streamlined shape. There are no windows for the rider to see the road. Instead, the rider steers by video screen, seeing through two small cameras on top of the bike.

AeroVelo's Eta bicycle reached a speed of 89.58 mph (144.17 kph).

The gear shifters action the derailleur to change gears.

Brake levers on the handlebars are linked to brake discs and brake pads.

The handlebars turn the front wheel.

Shock absorbers slide up and down –using springs or air–as the bicycle travels over rough ground. This gives a smoother ride.

The frame is designed to spread the cyclist's weight across the bicycle wheels.

Knobbly tires give more grip when cycling over rough ground.

The chain is a loop of metal links. It transfers the power from the pedals to the back wheel.

The axle attaches the wheel to the frame and allows the wheel to spin.

CARS

It's hard to believe that cars have only been around since the end of the 19th century. In 1885, German engineer Karl Benz designed and built the Benz Patent-Motorwagen. It was the very first car to be powered by an internal combustion engine. Today, there are over a billion cars on the road.

Benz's three-wheeled car was made of steel and wood. It had a maximum speed of 9.9 mph (16 kph).

Front and rear wings work in the opposite way to aircraft wings—they keep the car stuck to the ground, which enables it to go around corners faster.

SUCK, SQUEEZE, BANG, BLOW!

Most gas cars are powered by an internal combustion engine. This is also known as the four-stroke engine, because a piston on the end of a crankshaft moves down and up inside a cylinder four times in every cycle, like this:

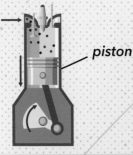

piston

1. The piston moves down to suck in a mixture of fuel and air.

2. The piston moves up to squeeze the air and fuel.

3. The mixture explodes with a bang, pushing the piston down again.

4. The piston moves up again to blow out the exhaust gases.

The cockpit is protected with a "halo" device. This safety feature helps protect the driver's head in a crash.

Rear wing

A Formula One car works in the same way as a gas-powered car. They both have internal combustion engines to make them move. They both have gears to change how fast the wheels spin. They both have steering wheels to change direction. The difference is that Formula One cars are designed to go a lot faster than normal cars. They are lightweight. Their engines are very powerful. And their aerodynamic shape means that they slip through the air easily.

Drivers change gear using paddles behind the steering wheel.

Tires are made from soft rubber to increase grip. They wear out quickly, so need to be changed during a race.

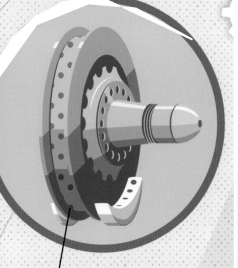

EXTREME ENGINEERING!

In 1997, ThrustSSC did more than set a new land-speed world record. It broke the sound barrier as well, to become the world's first supersonic car. ThrustSSC was powered by two jet engines and travelled faster than all current passenger aircraft!

Brake discs and pads are made from carbon fiber because this material can cope with the high temperatures generated when slowing down a car quickly.

ThrustSSC drove across Black Rock Desert in Nevada, USA at 763.035 mph (1227.985 kph).

TRUCKS

They're big, they're powerful and they're designed to transport cargo across land. Trucks are used to carry all sorts of goods, from milk and cookies to cars, houses, and even spacecraft. Some carry equipment and are used to do specialist jobs like firefighting.

mixer to the building site.

The water tank contains water used for making the concrete and for cleaning the truck after delivery.

Hydraulic motor to turn the drum

Axle

KEEP ON TRUCKING ...

There are two basic types of trucks—rigid and articulated. Rigid trucks are built as one unit, which includes both the driver's cab, the engine and the chassis. These are usually smaller. Articulated trucks can be very big and are made up of two units—the tractor and the trailer. The tractor contains the driver's cab (which often includes somewhere to sleep) and the engine. Different trailers can be attached to the tractors, so they can pull a variety of loads. But the heavier the load, the more axles a truck needs. This allows the weight to be divided between more wheels to avoid damaging the road. Really long articulated trucks have steerable wheels at the back as well as at the front!

Ladder to look into the drum and inspect the mix.

The loading hopper

The discharge chute is used to pour the concrete out.

IN THE MIX!

Cement mixers don't just transport cement to a construction site—they mix it too! The mixing is important, because it makes sure that the concrete doesn't set before it's needed.

EXTREME ENGINEERING!

Road trains are not trains at all, but trucks with very long trailers. Each one is made up of a tractor unit pulling two or more trailers. In 2006, the record for the world's longest road train was set in Australia by a vehicle that pulled 112 trailers and was nearly 1 mile (1.5 km) long.

Road trains are so heavy that it takes a long time for them to slow down. So if another vehicle is coming in the other direction, the best thing to do is just get out of the way!

TRAINS

Railway networks around the world are a great way of transporting both cargo and passengers. Did you know that it costs three times as much to carry cargo by road as it does by rail? Ropes, horses and gravity were first used to power trains as engines had not been invented yet. Horses were the first source of reliable power. Then steam power really got things going. Now, trains are usually powered by electricity or diesel.

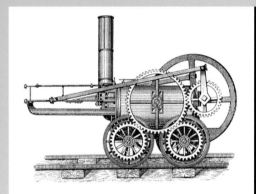

Richard Trevithick invented the steam locomotive in 1804.

Chimney

Cylinders containing the pistons

Valve gear was used to make the locomotive move backwards and forwards.

FULL STEAM AHEAD!

Steam engines turn coal into mechanical energy, which can be used to turn shafts and run different sorts of machines. Steam engines were used to provide power for factories during the Industrial Revolution (in the late 18th century). Then, at the beginning of the 19th century, steam power was first used to make trains move.

The way a steam locomotive works is very simple. A coal fire heats up water and, when it boils, this produces steam. The steam is forced into cylinders—one on each side of the locomotive—which each push a piston first one way and then the other. Each piston is connected to a driving rod, which is in turn connected to a driving wheel. As the pistons move back and forth, they turn the driving wheels and the steam locomotive moves.

EXTREME ENGINEERING!

Magnets are used to make Maglev trains move. Also known as bullet trains, they sit on a track that contains magnets that push the train up and propel it forwards. Because the train's wheels retract and it levitates on the magnetic field, there's no friction. This means that Maglev trains can travel much faster than normal trains.

Maglev trains can travel at speeds of over 373 mph (600 kph). That's three times faster than high-speed trains.

Coupling rods connected the wheels to make them turn together.

The boiler where the water is boiled to make steam.

Whistle

Driving cabin

The firebox where the coal is burnt.

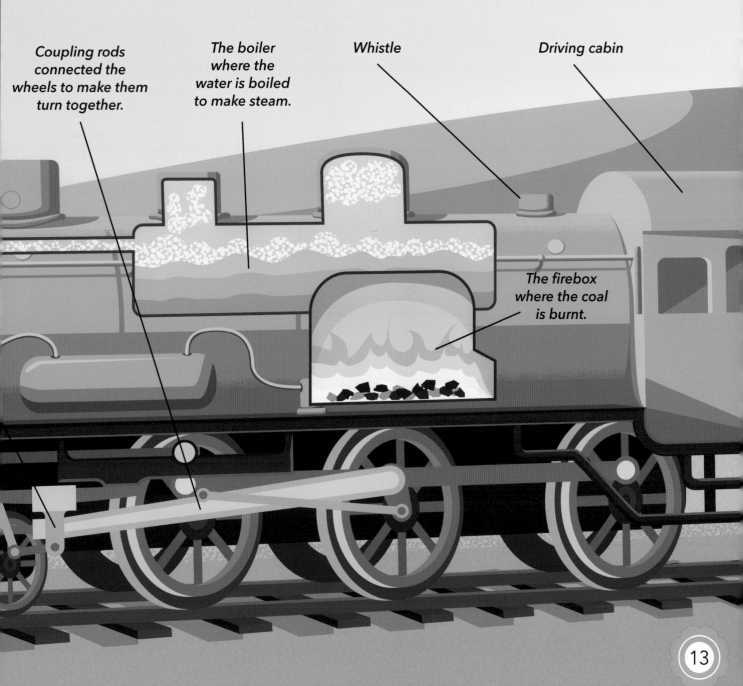

TANKS

A tank, also known as an armored car, is a machine used in battle. It is armed with weapons, while its super tough exterior protects the soldiers inside. However, it's the way a tank moves that really makes a difference on the battlefield. Its continuous track means that it can easily travel over very, very rough ground.

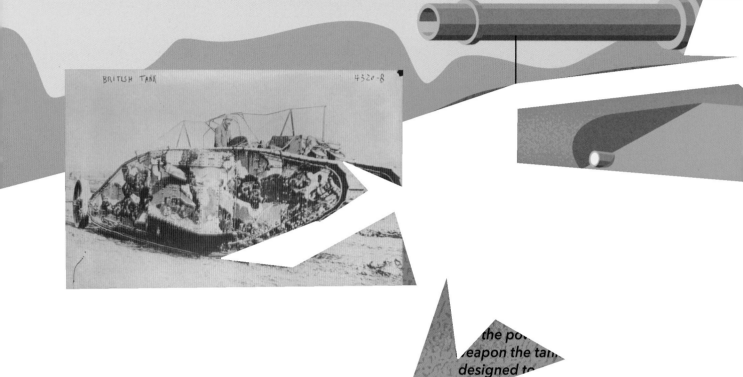

BRITISH TANK   4320-8

the po...
...eapon the tan...
designed t...

AROUND AND AROUND

Because of the weight of their armor, tanks can be extraordinarily heavy machines. This means that they need a powerful engine to make them move. Early tanks had internal combustion engines, like cars. But in newer models, gas turbine engines (also used in jet aircraft) are used to provide power.

Continuous tracks—usually known as caterpillar tracks—are used for two reasons. They spread out the weight of the tank so that it doesn't sink into the ground and get stuck. They also mean that ditches and obstacles are no problem! Caterpillar tracks are made up of hundreds of metal links. These travel round and round steel sprockets. Meanwhile, wheels run along the inside of the never-ending track.

The periscope lets the crew see.

Driver's hatch

The turret rotates to point the gun in different directions.

Caterpillar tracks

Tanks can drive just as quickly backwards as they can forwards, which makes them super maneuverable.

The drive sprocket drags the tracks under the wheels

EXTREME ENGINEERING!

The US Abrams is light, fast and easy to maneuver. It also uses revolutionary technology to repel attacks. When the Abrams is hit by a missile, the tank's armor actually explodes, pushing the missile away.

The Abrams' explosive reactive armor can be seen along the side of the tank—a series of rectangular blocks.

DIGGERS

It's often known as a "digger" but the real name for this familiar excavating machine is "backhoe loader." It's called this because of the action of the bucket at the back. Instead of picking material up and moving it forward, the bucket scoops back in the direction of the machine.

DIGGING DEEP

Excavators come in all shapes and sizes. Some have wheels, while others run on caterpillar tracks. A loader bucket at the front of a machine is used to pick up or push material. A backhoe is perfect for digging trenches. A backhoe loader is fixed to the end of an articulated arm, which bends like a real arm, allowing the backhoe bucket to reach awkward places. The arm works using hydraulic power, where liquid is used to move pistons.

The cab keeps the weather out but, more importantly, provides roll-over protection to the operator.

The loading bucket is used for picking up and moving piles of material.

The stabilizer legs are extended when the backhoe digs. They take the weight of the materials to avoid putting pressure on the wheels. Stabilizer legs are used to keep the digger level and hold it steady.

TOOLED UP

Excavators aren't always fitted with buckets or shovels. Different tools can be attached to the excavator to do specialist work: a breaker is used to hammer concrete or rock; a grapple is a claw used to grab material; and an auger is a drill used to make holes. Like the backhoe, these tools operate using hydraulics.

The backhoe operator swivels their seat around to use the backhoe!

The backhoe is used to dig trenches and deep holes.

EXTREME ENGINEERING!

A bucket-wheel excavator is a huge machine used in mining. It works like a fairground wheel, spinning to scoop bucket after bucket of material, which is whisked away on a conveyor belt.

Bagger 293 is a massive bucket-wheel excavator that can move nearly 8,828,667 cubic feet (250,000 cubic meters) of earth in just one day.

TOWER CRANES

If you've ever been past a big construction site, the chances are that you've seen a tower crane. And, as its name suggests, it probably towered over everything else. Tower cranes are perfect for lifting loads into places that are tricky to reach, quickly and easily.

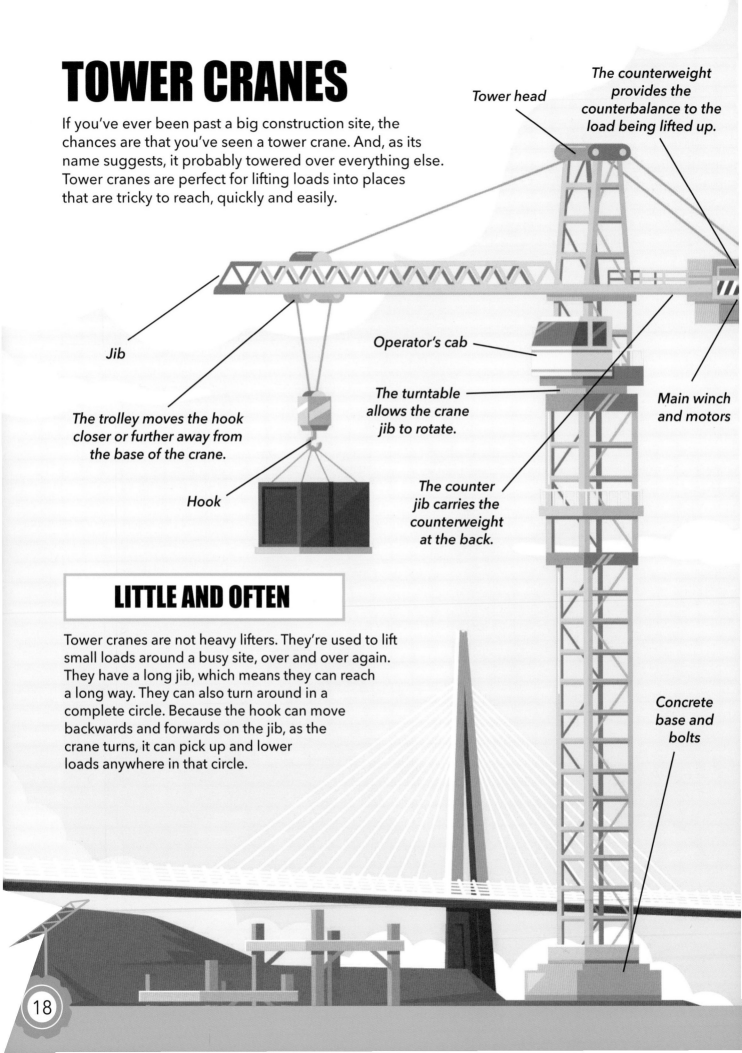

Tower head

The counterweight provides the counterbalance to the load being lifted up.

Jib

The trolley moves the hook closer or further away from the base of the crane.

Operator's cab

The turntable allows the crane jib to rotate.

Main winch and motors

Hook

The counter jib carries the counterweight at the back.

LITTLE AND OFTEN

Tower cranes are not heavy lifters. They're used to lift small loads around a busy site, over and over again. They have a long jib, which means they can reach a long way. They can also turn around in a complete circle. Because the hook can move backwards and forwards on the jib, as the crane turns, it can pick up and lower loads anywhere in that circle.

Concrete base and bolts

STANDING STILL

Tower cranes might look unstable, but they're not going anywhere in a hurry. Steel latticework means that each crane is strong, yet light. Meanwhile the bottom of the mast is securely fixed to a concrete base with bolts.

On bigger sites, builders might need more than one tower crane to cover the whole area.

GOING UP

Unlike mobile cranes, which are smaller and can be ready to use in just a few minutes, tower cranes can take days to put together. The crane is brought to the site in pieces. A mobile crane is used to build the jib, which is placed on top of a short mast. Then the tower crane uses hydraulic machinery to push itself upwards before slotting a new section of mast into the gap. It builds itself!

EXTREME ENGINEERING!

Super tall tower cranes are also used to build sky-high structures, like tower blocks and tall bridges. They were used to build the Millau Viaduct in France—the tallest bridge in the world.

The Millau Viaduct measures up to 1,125 feet (343 m) above the ground.

ent
too.

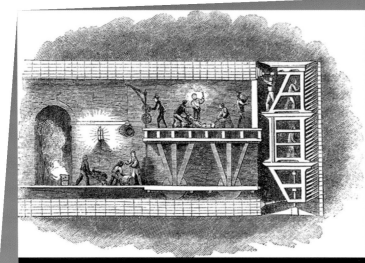

Sir Marc Isambard Brunel invented the tunneling shield in 1818. Construction workers could tunnel inside, safe from the danger of tunnel collapse.

The tunnel shield is the main body of the machine.

Screw conveyor

The cutterhead rotates, grinding away at the tunnel face to dig the tunnel.

SPINNING AROUND

TBMs are long, tube-shaped machines that move slowly underground, leaving a completed tunnel behind them. The cutterhead is a circular surface at the front of the machine covered with teeth. It spins, working like a huge cheese grater to chip away rock and soil.

This material is carried away from the tunnel face by a screw conveyor that picks the soil up from the bottom of the cutting head, lifts it behind the TBM's head and drops it on to a conveyor belt that transports it through the back of the TBM machine to the wagon loading area. Once the rail wagons are loaded, a train of wagons carries it out of the tunnel. The speed of the TBM varies; it travels slowly through hard rock and quickly through soft clay.

CONCRETE LINING

Tunnels are lined to make them super strong and prevent them from collapsing. As soon as the gap behind the cutterhead is big enough, the TBM slots in a ring of concrete segments. Hydraulic pistons push against the concrete ring to make sure that it fits snugly, while at the same time moving the TBM forward to do it all over again and again and again ...

Motors drive the cutter.

Rail tracks carry the concrete segments into the tunnel and waste material out.

The conveyor belt carries material out of the tunnel.

Concrete segments are fitted behind the tunnel shield to form the lining of the tunnel.

EXTREME ENGINEERING!

Bertha was one of the biggest TBMs ever. It was used to build a tunnel beneath the US city of Seattle big enough for a double-decker highway. The tunnel was 1.7 miles (2.7 km) long and opened in 2019.

Bertha's cutterhead had a diameter of 57 feet (17.4 m).

SEGMENTAL BRIDGE LAUNCHING MACHINES

Bridges are amazing structures that make it easier to travel from one place to another. They cross obstacles like valleys and rivers. But because bridges are often built in awkward places, they can cost a lot of money and take a long time to build. Now, segmental bridge launching machines are changing the way large structures are constructed.

HOW THEY WORK

Segmental bridge launching machines can build viaducts and elevated railways very, very quickly. Instead of standing on the ground like a crane, they sit on top of the structure they are building. They are perfect for building structures that have many identical bridge spans, which can be constructed on the ground and then lifted into place.

The segmental bridge launching machine straddles the gap between the first pillars. Then, bridge deck segments are lifted from the ground or passed along the machine and hung in place. When all the segments are hanging in a row, they are threaded with cables and tightened up, turning them into a solid bridge deck. The segmental bridge launching machine is disconnected from the new deck and, acting as a cantilever, is pushed out across the next span. This process is repeated again and again until the bridge is complete.

The main truss spans the gaps between the pillars. Bridge deck segments are hung from here.

Front and rear support legs provide temporary support while the main truss is extended across the gaps.

Bridge deck segments are threaded together to form each span of the new deck.

EXTREME ENGINEERING!

The SLJ900/32 is a monster of a machine. It's 298 feet (91 m) long, 23 feet (7 m wide), weighs 1,278,681 pounds (580 T) and runs on 64 wheels. Rather than slotting in small segments of pre-cast concrete, it lowers entire sections of bridge deck into position.

The SLJ900/32 is used to construct elevated rail viaducts.

The winch lifts the segments into place one by one.

Front and rear lower cross beams support the main truss when the new bridge deck is being constructed.

SNOW MACHINES

Many brilliant machines have been designed for when conditions are snowy. Snowplows and snow blowers are used to clear snowdrifts. Snowmobiles and skibobs are for whizzing over snow. And snow machines can be used to make snow!

Air nozzles direct compressed air into the water stream to blast it into many tiny water droplets.

SHIFTING SNOW

A snowplow is a large, wide blade that is designed to scrape a road clear of snow. The blade is placed on the road at an angle so that the snow shoots off to the side of the road, rather than landing back on it. Some snowplows are V-shaped, clearing snow away on both sides. They can be attached to vehicles including cars, trucks, tractors and even trains.

The fan spins to blow new snow high into the air.

The water supply provides the water to be turned into ice crystals.

Water nozzles spray water into the air which freezes around the ice pellets and starts to form snow.

MAKING SNOW

Snow machines (pictured)—or snow cannons—are used to make artificial snow. Real snow forms high in the atmosphere, where molecules of water vapor meet specks of dust and freeze to form six-sided ice crystals. These grow larger and heavier until they fall as snowflakes. Snow machines work quite differently. Compressed air and water are combined at high speed, to create tiny water droplets and blow them into the air. When the pressure drops suddenly, so does the temperature to create tiny balls of snow. Once they land, both real and artificial snow look the same!

EXTREME ENGINEERING!

A snowmobile is a small powered vehicle designed to travel over snow and ice. It has an internal combustion engine, like a motorcycle, but runs on tracks. The small skis can be turned to steer the snowmobile.

Some snowmobiles are so powerful that their riders can perform jumps and somersaults!

The air compressor is used to pressurize the water system and nozzles.

PERSONAL TRANSPORTERS

Some of the very newest inventions have been built for just one person to ride. Segways, electric skateboards, electric kick scooters, self-balancing unicycles and self-balancing scooters are all types of personal transporter. They are designed for travel, but mostly fun.

RECHARGEABLE ENERGY

Most personal transporters are powered by lithium-ion batteries. Lithium is lightweight, which means that it takes less energy to move. It can also hold a lot of electrical charge and provides electrical power for longer than other types of battery. Best of all, lithium-ion batteries are rechargeable.

BALANCING ACT

The human body is pretty good at staying upright. This is because movement of fluid in the inner ear tells the brain when it's out of balance and in danger of falling. When it receives this information, the brain tells the body to change position until it's balanced once more. Personal transporters use this idea to move. Gyroscopes inside the machine are used to register its position, while the motor turns the wheels at exactly the right speed to keep the rider moving without falling flat on their face, or their back.

EXTREME ENGINEERING!

Unlike traditional skateboards, Future Motion's electric skateboard has just one big wheel, which sits in the middle. OneWheel+ XR has a top speed of 18.6 mph (30 kph), a range of 18 miles (29 km) and can even go off-road!

It only takes 100 minutes to recharge this electric skateboard!

This scooter is operated using the handlebars. Pushing them forwards and backwards makes the scooter move back and forth. Turning the handlebars left or right makes the scooter change direction.

The motors are inside the wheels.

Batteries in the base keep the center of gravity low and make the scooter stand upright.

MORE MEGA MACHINES

CATERPILLAR 797

Caterpillar's 797 series of dump trucks is awesome. These giant off-road machines are used in mining and are built to carry up to 1,373,480 pounds (623 T) of material in one trip and then dump it, of course. That's over 20 times as much as a standard dump truck's load. It's also the same weight as 49 double-decker buses!

The Caterpillar 797F's top speed is 42 mph (68 kph)! Each tire is over 13 feet (4 m) tall!

MHI VESTAS V164

This enormous offshore wind turbine is designed to turn the wind's energy into electrical energy. The V164 is named after its rotor, which has a diameter of 538 feet (164 m). Each blade weighs 7,161 pounds (35 T)!

It's estimated that each V164 wind turbine can power nearly 6,000 homes.

MARION 8050 DRAGLINE

A walking dragline excavator is a cross between a crane and an excavator. It carries a bucket on the end of its extra-long boom and uses this to scoop up and move material. But the Marion 8050 goes one step further, literally. It moves by walking —sliding its long steel walking shoes forwards or backwards.

The Marion 8050 is used in open-cast mining.

NASA'S CRAWLER-TRANSPORTER 2 (C-T2)

Have you ever wondered how a spacecraft gets from the building where it is made to the launchpad? This is a job for a crawler-transporter like CT-2—a huge, tracked vehicle with a flat, square deck. Don't expect CT-2 to travel very fast though. It might be able to carry over 17,636,982 pounds (8,000 T), but its top speed is just 0.9 mph (1.6 kph).

CT-2 was first used in 1966. It's now been upgraded to carry the new Space Launch System (SLS).

GLOSSARY

aerodynamic
having a shape that makes moving through air easier

atmosphere
the mixture of gases around Earth

axle
a bar connected to the center of a wheel that allows it to turn

boom
a long pole that moves

bridge deck
the surface of a bridge; cars and trains travel on this

cantilever
a beam that is supported at only one end and sticks outwards

carbon fiber
a material that is very light, yet very strong and resistant to high temperatures

cargo
goods carried on a ship, aircraft or motor vehicle

compressed
squeezed

counterbalance
a weight that balances another weight

crankshaft
a long metal rod that helps an engine turn the wheels

diesel
a type of fuel

friction
the force that makes it difficult for one object to slide along the surface of another or to move through a liquid or gas

fuel
a substance that is used to provide heat or power, usually by being burned

gear
a device used to control the speed of wheels

gyroscope
a spinning device that shows when something has changed direction

hydraulic
when something is operated using a liquid

internal combustion engine
a type of engine; it burns fuel to make machines like cars and motorcycle move

jib
a long horizontal frame that sticks out from a crane and from which the hook hangs

latticework
strips of wood or other material that cross over each other with spaces in between

lever
a bar that can be used to make it easier to move something heavy

levitate
to rise in the air

lithium
a lightweight silvery metal

magnetic field
the space around a magnet where its force can attract or repel magnetic materials

maneuver
to turn and direct an object

periscope
a long, vertical tube containing a set of mirrors that gives you a view of what is above you when you look through the bottom of the tube

piston
an engine part, which moves up and down or forwards and backwards

pulley
a wheel with a groove around the edge; when a rope is run around the pulley, it can be used to lift things

rotor
a set of blades

segmental
something that is divided into segments or pieces

shock absorber
a device that reduces the effects of travelling over rough or uneven ground

sprocket
a device like a wheel with one or more rows of tooth-like parts sticking out that keeps a chain moving

streamlined
designed in a way that makes movement easier through air or water

supersonic
faster than the speed of sound

trench
a narrow hole that is dug into the ground

truss
a metal structure or frame

viaduct
a long bridge that carries cars or trains across a valley

winch
a machine that lifts heavy objects by turning a chain or rope around a tube-shaped device

WEBSITES

sciencemuseum.org.uk
Find out more about the Science Museum in London, the home of many transport-based exhibits.

explainthatstuff.com/historyofcars.html
More information about the history of cars.

wonderopolis.org/wonder/how-does-a-crane-work
Build your own crane!

bicycle-and-bikes.com/history-of-bicycles/
A history of bicycles.

www.youtube.com/watch?v=190eH_AJeWQ
Watch a video of SLJ900/32 segmental bridge launching machine in action.

BOOKS

The Ultimate Book of Vehicles
by Anne-Sophie Baumann (Chronicle Books, 2014)

Car Science
by Richard Hammond (DK Children, 2011)

Awesome Engineering: Trains, Planes and Ships
by Sally Spray (Franklin Watts, 2017)

Big Book of Machines
by Minna Lacey (Usborne, 2017)

Stickmen's Guide to Gigantic Machines
by John Farndon and John Paul de Quay (Hungry Tomato, 2016)

Mega Machine Record Breakers
by Anne Rooney (Carlton Publishing, 2019)

INDEX